SACRAMENTO PUBLIC LIBRARY

3 3029 05771 9445

SACRAMENTO PUBLIC LIBRARY
828 "I" STREET
SACRAMENTO, CA 95814

11/2006

D0461598

WITHDRAWN FROM
CIRCULATION

Máquinas maravillosas/Mighty Machines

Barredoras de calles/Street Sweepers

por/by Terri DeGezelle

Traducción/Translation: Dr. Martín Luis Guzmán Ferrer
Editor Consultor/Consulting Editor: Dra. Gail Saunders-Smith

Consultor/Consultant: Amy Allen, Administrative Director
North American Power Sweeping Association
Kalamazoo, Michigan

Capstone
press®

Mankato, Minnesota

Pebble Plus is published by Capstone Press,
151 Good Counsel Drive, P.O. Box 669, Mankato, Minnesota 56002.
www.capstonepress.com

Copyright © 2007 by Capstone Press. All rights reserved.
No part of this publication may be reproduced in whole or in part, or stored in a retrieval system, or
transmitted in any form or by any means, electronic, mechanical, photocopying, recording, or otherwise,
without written permission of the publisher. For information regarding permission, write to Capstone Press,
151 Good Counsel Drive, P.O. Box 669, Dept. R, Mankato, Minnesota 56002.
Printed in the United States of America

1 2 3 4 5 6 11 10 09 08 07 06

Library of Congress Cataloging-in-Publication Data
DeGezelle, Terri, 1955–
    [Street sweepers. Spanish & English]
    Barredoras de calles = Street sweepers/de Terri DeGezelle.
    p. cm.—(Pebble plus. Máquinas maravillosas = Pebble plus. Mighty machines)
    Includes index.
    ISBN-13: 978-0-7368-6675-0 (hardcover)
    ISBN-10: 0-7368-6675-2 (hardcover)
    1. Street cleaning—Equipment and supplies—Juvenile literature. 2. Street cleaning—Juvenile literature.
3. Trucks—Juvenile literature. I. Title: Street sweepers. II. Title. III. Pebble plus. Máquinas maravillosas. IV.
Pebble plus. Mighty machines.
TD860.D4418 2007
629.225—dc22   2005037465

Summary: Simple text and photographs present street sweeperes, their parts, and their jobs—in both English
    and Spanish.

Editorial Credits
Martha E. H. Rustad, editor; Katy Kudela, bilingual editor; Eida del Risco, Spanish copy editor; Molly Nei,
    set designer; Ted Williams, book designer; Wanda Winch, photo researcher; Scott Thoms, photo editor

Photo Credits
Capstone Press/Karon Dubke, cover, 1, 8–9, 10–11, 12–13, 15, 16–17, 21; Daniel E. Hodges, 7; The Image Works/
Mark Antman, 19; PhotoEdit Inc./Thomas Michael Corcoran, 5

The author thanks Bernie Fasnacht, Street Foreman, City of Mankato, Minnesota, for his assistance with this
book. Pebble Plus thanks the City of Mankato (Minnesota) Street Division for assistance with photo shoots.

Note to Parents and Teachers

The Máquinas maravillosas/Mighty Machines set supports national standards related to
science, technology, and society. This book describes street sweepers in both English and
Spanish. The images support early readers in understanding the text. The repetition of
words and phrases helps early readers learn new words. This book also introduces early
readers to subject-specific vocabulary words, which are defined in the Glossary section.
Early readers may need assistance to read some words and to use the Table of Contents,
Glossary, Internet Sites, and Index sections of the book.

Table of Contents

Tabla de contenidos

A Street Sweeper's Job

A street sweeper cleans
paved streets and highways.
Clean streets are safer
and last longer than dirty streets.

Cómo trabaja una barredora de calles

Las barredoras de calles limpian
las calles pavimentadas y las carreteras.
Las calles limpias son más seguras y
duran más que las calles sucias.

Parts of Street Sweepers

Street sweepers have
big turning brushes.
Brushes sweep dirt and
garbage into hoppers.

Las partes de las barredoras de calles

Las barredoras de calles tienen
grandes cepillos que giran.
Los cepillos barren la tierra y
la basura y la meten en una tolva.

brush/cepillo

Some street sweepers use air.

Air blows dirt toward the brushes.

Vacuums suck the dirt into the hopper.

Algunas barredoras de calles
usan aire. El aire mueve la tierra
hacia los cepillos. La aspiradora
mete la tierra dentro de la tolva.

**vacuum/
aspiradora**

Hoppers fill up with dirt
and garbage.
Drivers dump full hoppers
into garbage trucks.

Las tolvas se llenan con tierra
y basura. Los conductores
descargan las tolvas llenas
en los camiones de la basura.

hopper/tolva

Sweeping makes dust.
Street sweepers have sprayers
that wash away dust.

Al barrer se crea polvo.
Las barredoras de calles tienen
rociadores que quitan el polvo.

sprayer/rociador

sprayer/rociador

13

What Street Sweepers Do

Street sweepers clean gutters.

In the summer,

they sweep up

dirt and garbage.

Qué hacen las barredoras de calles

Las barredoras de calles

limpian las alcantarillas.

En el verano, quitan

la tierra y la basura.

In the fall, street sweepers
pick up leaves.
They also sweep up
after parades.

En el otoño, las barredoras
de calles recogen las hojas.
También barren después
de los desfiles.

In the winter, sand and salt
build up on streets and highways.
In the spring, street sweepers
clean dirty streets.

En el invierno, la arena y la sal
se juntan en las calles y carreteras.
En la primavera, las barredoras de
calles limpian las calles sucias.

Mighty Street Sweepers

All year round, street sweepers

keep streets clean and safe for travel.

Street sweepers are mighty machines.

Maravillosas barredoras de calles

Durante todo el año, las barredoras

de calles mantienen la calles limpias

y seguras. Las barredoras de calles

son unas máquinas maravillosas.

Glossary

brush—a tool with long hairs called bristles

garbage—trash and other items people throw away

gutter—a space next to the curb where rain drains away from a street

hopper—a large container on a street sweeper that holds dirt and garbage

parade—a long line of people and vehicles that are part of a ceremony or festival

sprayer—a tool that shoots out water

travel—going from one place to another

vacuum—a machine that cleans by sucking up dirt

Glosario

la alcantarilla—espacio junto a la acera por donde se mete la lluvia que cae en la calle

la aspiradora—máquina que limpia aspirando el polvo

la basura—desperdicios y otras cosas que tiran las personas

el cepillo—herramienta con unos pelos largos que se llaman cerdas

el desfile—formación larga de personas y vehículos que son parte de una ceremonia o fiesta

el rociador—dispositivo que esparce agua

la tolva—recipiente grande donde las barredoras ponen tierra y basura

viajar—ir de un lugar a otro

Internet Sites

FactHound offers a safe, fun way to find Internet sites related to this book. All of the sites on FactHound have been researched by our staff.

Here's how:

1. Visit *www.facthound.com*

2. Choose your grade level.

3. Type in this book ID **0736866752** for age-appropriate sites. You may also browse subjects by clicking on letters, or by clicking on pictures and words.

4. Click on the **Fetch It** button.

FactHound will fetch the best sites for you!

Index

air, 8	hoppers, 6, 8, 10
brushes, 6, 8	leaves, 16
dirt, 6, 8, 10, 14	safety, 4, 20
drivers, 10	salt, 18
dust, 12	sand, 18
garbage, 6, 10, 14	sprayers, 12
garbage trucks, 10	streets, 4, 18, 20
gutters, 14	vacuums, 8
highways, 4, 18	

Sitios de Internet

FactHound proporciona una manera divertida y segura de encontrar sitios de Internet relacionados con este libro. Nuestro personal ha investigado todos los sitios de FactHound. Es posible que los sitios no estén en español.

Se hace así:

1. Visita *www.facthound.com*

2. Elige tu grado escolar.

3. Introduce este código especial **0736866752** para ver sitios apropiados según tu edad, o usa una palabra relacionada con este libro para hacer una búsqueda general.

4. Haz clic en el botón **Fetch It**.

¡FactHound buscará los mejores sitios para ti!

Índice

aire, 8	cepillos, 6, 8
alcantarillas, 14	conductores, 10
arena, 18	hojas, 16
aspiradora, 8	polvo, 12
basura, 6, 10, 14	rociadores, 12
calles, 4, 18, 20	sal, 18
camiones de la basura, 10	seguridad, 4, 20
	tierra, 6, 8, 10, 14
carreteras, 4, 18	tolva, 6, 8, 10